Modise Tlharesagae

SABBATH:

THE BASIC

VERSION

Modise Tlharesagae/**SABBATH: THE BASIC VERSION©**
2020

Contact Address: Modise Tlharesagae
P O Box 10552
Kanye
Botswana
E-mail address:
tlharesage@gmail.com

Contact number: (0267) 73 183 747
(0267) 77 461 935
(0267) 71 901 489
(0267) 544 33 55

Cover design: Bobby David Ideas

Sabbath: The Basic Version © 2020

Unless and otherwise stated scriptures are quoted from the King James Version (KJV) of the Holy Bible. All other language words are Greek for all New Testment and Hebrew for all Old Testment words. It is thus as the New Testment manuscripts were translated from Greek and closer languages and Old Testment from Hebrew manuscripts making it easy to search the right meaning of the word from its originally written language

Table of

Contents

Prologue

One of the grand and best kept secrets of the Christian fraternity is the **Sabbath**. This being the product of the revelation availed to Prophet Moses; the Lord did not indwell the reason why the congregation had to keep His tradition of keeping the Sabbath. But rather He just gave Moses the simplistic definition; "...because I have finished my work on the Friday and rested on the Sabbath," but we hear a totally new interpretation in the book of Hebrews, that who has entered the real Sabbath is done with matters of this world. Meaning what is kept here on earth is the shadow of what God did in keeping the Sabbath.

What usually pains understanding is the concerted meaning of the authoring and implementation of the Sabbath day here on earth. Is it enough to just sanctify a day for a memorial just because we finished our work on it? Or was there a deeper meaning to it than met the revelation given Moses. Yet a more profound question is would you agree to a temporary covenant in keeping a shadow of the truth? Then it seems fit that

Israel could not be told the real meaning for it would define the stone covenant a temporal measure whereas there is the actual that shall be kept by all.

HEBREWS 8:10 KJV

For this is the covenant that I will make with the house of Israel after those days, saith the Lord; I will put my laws into their mind, and write them in their hearts: and I will be to them a God, and they shall be to me a people:

My compounded study of the subject matter of the Sabbath also revealed a startling truth, that because of the sin nature of this realm that we have been redeemed of, we cannot have our real Sabbath here nor eternal life. That is why the Lord says in the next life or when we have entered the real Sabbath or His rest, shall we then be given eternal life. In other words, as He had to lose His life for Him to enter the true Holy of Holies, so are we; to be the children of the resurrection to partake of both the permanent rest and to have the life eternal.

MARK 10:30 KJV

But he shall receive an hundredfold now in

this time, houses, and brethren, and sisters, and mothers, and children, and lands, with persecutions; **and in the world to come eternal life.**

Until we are serious about understanding the things of God, God cannot reveal the riches of His kingdom to us. So as we simply keep or not keep the Sabbath, without seeking out its true meaning, or just believe we have eternal life not knowing whether in this world or the world to come, we become babes tossed to and fro by the cunning craftiness of men, but we need to grow in Him in all things.

EPHESIANS 4:10-15 KJV

He that descended is the same also that ascended up far above all heavens, that he might fill all things.) And he gave some, apostles; and some, prophets; and some, evangelists; and some, pastors and teachers; For the perfecting of the saints, for the work of the ministry, for the edifying of the body of Christ: Till we all come in the unity of the faith, and of the knowledge of the Son of God, unto a perfect man, unto the measure of the stature of the fulness of Christ: That we henceforth be no more children, tossed to and fro, and carried about with every wind of doctrine, by the sleight of men, and cunning craftiness, whereby they lie in wait to deceive; But speaking the truth in love, may grow up into him in all things, which is the head, even Christ:

Sincerely, it is not about how many others believe with you what you believe, but it is about the truth and sincerity it carries before God that matters most. And God though pitiful does not govern by pity but principle. Meaning if you followed the rest, you will perish with the rest.

HOSEA 4:6 KJV
My people are destroyed for lack of knowledge: because thou hast rejected knowledge, I will also reject thee, that thou shalt be no priest to me: seeing thou hast forgotten the law of thy God, I will also forget thy children.

In pursuing the truth about the Sabbath one soon finds out that the Sabbath is not a day, but the day is a commemoration here on earth. If then the day be a memorial, then it is much more important to know what the day commemorates so that in keeping or not keeping it, we may know why it was initiated to be kept and why it has or should not be kept?

This does not just help us understand the Sabbath or the eternal realm, but it also helps us understand all the scriptures and revelations that are related to the Sabbath. The Holy Bible says they shall know the truth and the truth shall set them free, even as Christ came preaching deliverance, we ought to know the real truth to be free indeed.

JOHN 8:32 KJV

And ye shall know the truth, and the truth shall make you free.

LUKE 4:18 KJV

*The Spirit of the Lord is upon me, because he hath anointed me to preach the gospel to the poor; he hath sent me to heal the brokenhearted, **to preach deliverance to the captives**, and recovering of sight to the blind, to set at liberty them that are bruised,*

With that said and done. When the Lord says He is going to prepare us a place, it would easily relate to why we did not have a place in heaven until He had redeemed us. For if He had to go before us to prepare a place for us, it simply means before He came we did not have a place in heaven or eternity.

JOHN 14:2 KJV
In my Father's house are many mansions: if it were not so, I would have told you. I go to prepare a place for you.

Understanding this scripture is a thing only available to a person who understands the meaning and the purpose of the Sabbath day, and the place of our eternal rest. God had separated Himself in to a place that we would be able to get in to only when we have been redeemed. Abraham and all the Old Covenant saints could not appear before God or come in to His presence until the Sabbath was fulfilled. That is why they were kept captives in Abraham's bosom in the belly of the earth until Christ broke the veil in heaven and on earth. Until the way in to the true Holy Place was given to man by His own blood of redemption.

LUKE 16:22-23 KJV
And it came to pass, that the beggar died,

and was carried by the angels into Abraham's bosom: the rich man also died, and was buried; And in hell he lift up his eyes, being in torments, and seeth Abraham afar off, and Lazarus in his bosom.

Until and unless we understand the mystery of Sabbath, we cannot understand why Abraham and those saints had to endure the screams of the torment of those in hell as their neighbors in waiting.

HEBREWS 4:1-11 KJV

Let us therefore fear, lest, a promise being left us of entering into his rest, any of you should seem to come short of it. For unto us was the gospel preached, as well as unto them: but the word preached did not profit them, not being mixed with faith in them that heard it. For we which have believed do enter into rest, as he said, As I have sworn in my wrath, if they shall enter into my rest: although the works were finished from the foundation of the world. For he spake in a certain place of the seventh day on this wise, And God did rest the seventh day from all his works. And in this place again, If they shall enter into my rest. Seeing therefore it remaineth that some must enter therein, and *they to whom it was first preached entered not in because of unbelief: Again, he limiteth a certain day, saying in David, To day, after so long a time; as it is said, To day if ye will hear his voice, harden not your hearts. **For if Jesus had given them rest**, then would he not afterward have spoken of another day. There remaineth therefore a rest to the people of God. For he that is entered into his rest, he also hath ceased from his own works, as God did from his. Let us labour therefore to enter into that rest, lest any man fall after the same example of unbelief.*

In the above text we gather that, the Sabbath as entered in on earth is the shadow of a place where man or the children of God joins Him in heaven, only after completing their earthly journey. It clearly shows that the actual Sabbath is not a day but a place of rest. Meaning when people usually say Jesus is their Sabbath it is wrong and deceitful, but the Sabbath is a place we enter when we are done with the matters of this world.

The other key thing that we gather from the above text is only when we have exit this world shall we enter the real Sabbath.

Meaning it is a certain place where God have separated himself from us, so that we may follow Him there. Meaning there was or is a place where God entered in to for the sake of separation, so that at the right time we may join Him there.

Yet most presumably, all seem to have a reason to shun or to keep the Sabbath but none seems to know why? The Charismatic church, the Pentecostal church, the Baptist church, Presbyterian church and a number other denominations will simply tell you Christ is their Sabbath which is not true according to **HEBREWS 4:1-11**, for the Holy Bible says: Sabbath or God's rest is a place the redeemed enter on the condition of faith or believe. None the less, the Jesus is my Sabbath excuse is a good reason that can hold water in contention tact until we bring in scripture, for the Lord Himself did not call Himself the Sabbath, but generally everyone calls Him their Sabbath, which contradicts His statement about the Sabbath.

The Lord when asked why He does not keep the Sabbath or encourage His disciples to keep it said to those who beckoned to Him that He is the Lord of the Sabbath, meaning

He is above the Sabbath, for the Sabbath was made for man.

MARK 2:28 KJV
Therefore the Son of man is Lord also of the sabbath.

MATTHEW 12:8 KJV
For the Son of man is Lord even of the sabbath day.

LUKE 6:5 KJV
And he said unto them, That the Son of man is Lord also of the sabbath.

The ideal that He does not say this once, but **thrice** in the same context in the gospels gives us the clarity; this **reiteration** does not only prove that indeed the three writers being direct witnesses have heard Him say He is the Lord of the Sabbath; and He did not say He is the Sabbath, but it also proves the accuracy of the account, that indeed He is the Lord of the Sabbath, not the Sabbath.

Having said that, it is ideal to then look and see clearly through scripture and revelation of scripture, what is the Sabbath? Its purpose, and its operation through the

Chronicles of Orders and Covenants; starting from the inception in the times of Adam.

The ideal of this book is not about why we have to keep the Sabbath or whether we should keep the Sabbath, but it is a simple account of what the Sabbath is. Its origination and its actual keeping. Its use under the three Orders; Luciferian, Melchisedec and the Christ Order. The most yearning question that one could ask about the Sabbath is; why? Why was the Sabbath incepted? Yet the most taunting question is why it had to be kept even by God Himself? To bring to clarity this travail of ages, one should first try to understand what caused God to even incept the Sabbath, and here the whole story begins to unravel this mystery.

The key thing to remember is it was the seventh day here on earth when God the Father entered in to the Sabbath, or separated Himself from the affairs or the activities of this earth. In simple terms, He cast all things earthly; rule and dominion, in to the hands of Adam and Eve. The key principle being, when we say He entered the Sabbath, we mean He left the affairs of this world to man. And His entering in to the Sabbath, meant he left a memorial day for the inhabitants of the earth. Meaning we have to be exceeding sure and clear that, it meant Adam and Eve had to kept the Sabbath, for it was sanctified here on earth for a memorial before them.

HEBREWS 4:10 KJV

For he that is entered into his rest, he also hath ceased from his own works, as God did from his.

The inception of Sabbath here on earth meant a New Order in heaven, for there are no days or nights in the third heaven, but in the eternal realm is a vast expanse of God's glory, which meant a totally different instance.

2PETER 3:8 KJV

But, beloved, be not ignorant of this one thing, that one day is with the Lord as a thousand years, and a thousand years as one day.

This meant that though Sabbath was a memorial day on earth, it was an Order (research: **THE CHRONICLES OF ORDER** or get **THE PRINCIPLE OF ORDER** by same author) in heaven; with a sanctuary, better known as the tabernacle of testimony, to make God a separate entity from all forms of the created in heaven and on earth (by getting Him in to the Holy of Holies in heaven), the Sabbath meant a cessation of God's service here on earth. So there was one who accessed His presence, according to the occasion where there is a need for that. And Melchisedec was the High Priest of that Order; being the pre-incarnate Christ. The same Holy of Holies that Christ as the High Priest of the New Covenant entered, bearing the price of redemption; His own blood.

HEBREWS 9:24 KJV

For Christ is not entered into the holy places made with hands, which are the figures of the true; but into heaven itself, now to appear in the presence of God for us:

In simple terms, God imprisoned Himself, so that if man commit any form of wrong; sin, He may not appear or enter His presence until redeemed. Or so that man may not sin in His presence, so that man's sin unlike the devil's sin may not be eternal. To make it sound simpler, the devil sinned in the presence of God, meaning his sin was carried out in the eternal realm, making it perpetual or eternal. And according to principle irreversible. So immediately after appreciating the beauty of the restored earth, and after making Adam and Eve its custodians, God Himself went in to separation, and left the seventh day a memorial of holiness to them.

Then if He went in to separation, it meant He had to be reached through someone. Thus there was a need for a priest, to wait before the Holy of Holies in heaven, where God in His eternal glory had to be contained or imprisoned for the sake of man until a fitting approval has been reached about man's ability to conquer or be defeated by sin. In simple terms, when God had created man, He granted man freewill, with the blessed assurance that he will be tested to pass or fail, but the Sabbath separated Him from the works of man so that man may not sin or fall in His eternal presence.

The seventh day was thus sanctified from the beginning, as a memorial or reminder that man has to be holy or live a holy life. But in heaven it was actually happening, the tabernacle was set, with God in its Holiest of places/ Most Holy place or Holy of Holies, and a priest to wait on God and to relay the messages of the messengers about the affairs of the earth through Him.

GENESIS 14:18 KJV

*And Melchizedek king of Salem brought forth bread and wine: and he was **the priest of the most high** God.*

Before the earthly congregation of Israel or their tabernacle was set in place, we thus discover this profound truth about what was already happening in heaven, God had His own priest called Melchizedek.

EXODUS 25:9 KJV

According to all that I shew thee, after the pattern of the tabernacle, and the pattern of all the instruments thereof, even so shall ye make it.

HEBREWS 9:24 KJV

For Christ is not entered into the holy places made with hands, which are the figures of the true; but into heaven itself, now to appear in the presence of God for us:

The Sabbath is thus not just a significant day kept on earth, but was a form of preservation for man. It was incepted so that man may have a memorial of Holiness and may have a way out in case he fails. In simple terms, the Sabbath was not made for God, but for the sake of man. So that as he goes through his earthly trial and error moment, he may also have a way out in case he sins.

MARK 2:27 KJV

And he said unto them, The sabbath was made for man, and not man for the sabbath:

The common mistake of the New Testament believers is that they often mistake the Sabbath to have begun with the Mosaic Law here on earth, but the Sabbath was here way before the Law. The Sabbath was sanctified way before the Stone Covenant. This meaning that, God even before Moses built an earthly sanctuary, was already separated from the heavenly creatures. That is why, when Christ has been crucified and resurrected, he enters the Holy of Holies not built by hands, meaning as Aaron entered in to the Holy of Holies to access God once a year, there was also a kind of original pattern he was taking after. That is why when Moses builds the earthly sanctuary, it has to be built **after** or in the likeness of the actual one in heaven.

EXODUS 25:9 KJV

*According to all that I shew thee, **after the pattern of the tabernacle**, and the pattern of all the instruments thereof, even so shall ye make it.*

The building of the Mosaic tabernacle **after** the pattern of the tabernacle that is in heaven, gives us an understanding that if there be the actual original in heaven, with the Holiest place, it meant the Sabbath here on earth was a memorial of the original separation that God had entered for us.

So this separation of holiness, was to be a memorial for the coming things too. It meant God even before Moses built a tabernacle here on earth, He prepared Himself one to separate Himself from even the heavenly creatures. The other key thing is Adam and Eve had to also partake for in heaven there are no days. If the seventh day had to be made holy, it meant here on earth.

One has to observe carefully that, not only God had to partake of the Sabbath. Also the inhabitants of the earth where the day has been sanctified had to partake. But it meant the whole earth had to partake on the seventh day here on earth but there was an introduction of a tabernacle of rest in heaven. And in the latter times when here on earth there was a memorial mercy seat in the tabernacle of Moses; there in heaven the Father all along had been seated on a real mercy seat in the real Holy of Holies.

The reason the Mosaic Covenant, or the Covenant of Tablets of Stone is called the Shadow Covenant, it is because whatever Aaron did here on earth, had to be repeated by Melchizedek in heaven before God in the true Holy of Holies.

The Sabbath

One profound thing we have to quickly clear is that Jesus is not the Sabbath, yet again! He says I shall give you rest, or Sabbath. By so saying, He does not direct us to Himself as the Sabbath, but the Sabbath as something that is in His hand or control, and that He can give to someone.

MATTHEW 11:28 KJV

Come unto me, all ye that labour and are heavy laden, and I will give you rest.

Yet another profound statement the Lord said is that the Sabbath was created for the sake of man. Meaning there was a need for God to abscond, or set self aside from the matters of humanity so that they may be able to exercise freewill.

MARK 2:27 KJV

And he said unto them, The sabbath was made for man, and not man for the sabbath:

That way it allowed God to determine whether man can live his life as an autonomous or a semi-autonomous being. By being granted all things, man was granted the right to have dominion over all things not just once but twice.

GENESIS 1:28 KJV

And God blessed them, and God said unto them, Be fruitful, and multiply, and replenish the earth, and subdue it: and have dominion over the fish of the sea, and over the fowl of the air, and over every living thing that moveth upon the earth.

GENESIS 9:1-3 KJV

And God blessed Noah and his sons, and said unto them, Be fruitful, and multiply, and replenish the earth. And the fear of you and the dread of you shall be upon every beast of the earth, and upon every fowl of the air, upon all that moveth upon the earth, and upon all the fishes of the sea; into your hand are they delivered. Every moving thing that liveth shall be meat for you; even as the green herb have I given you all things.

After God dealt away with all the scums of the world through the flood of Noah, He afforded and accorded Noah a much better blessing well above that of Adam and Eve, but yet man failed to uphold.

In essence the Sabbath like I always presume was a more profound way to preserve us, there could have never been a better way. For as long as we sinned outside the realm of eternity we were hopeful that God has locked himself in a small place called the Holy of Holies so that we may if peradventure sin, we may commit sin out of His sight and eternity. So that we may have a doorway back in.

Where man has failed as an individual, God rose a nation in their stead, but the peculiar people also so failed God that He was bloated of their offerings and sacrifices. In simple terms, man could not just hold on to leadership unaided of God, autonomy was not his thing so it proved.

HEBREWS 10:5 KJV

Wherefore when he cometh into the world, he saith, Sacrifice and offering thou wouldest not, but a body hast thou prepared me:

Before we go in to the redemption of man, we must first really see in all clarity that for the sake of man, by subjecting Himself in to the Sabbath, God left the human affairs by separating humanity from His eternal presence and glory so that man may not fall in His presence in case he did fall.

GENESIS 3:11 KJV

And he said, Who told thee that thou wast naked? Hast thou eaten of the tree, whereof I commanded thee that thou shouldest not eat?

GENESIS 3:11, contrary to popular believe, the Lord did not test Adam when He asked him if he had eaten of the fruit of the tree

He had told him not to eat. He actually did not know, because of the Sabbath. He had sealed self from the affairs of man, so when it was time for fellowship, God as usual came to be in fellowship for He had sanctified a meeting day for Him and Adam's house, the Sabbath.

This determines that God had to be in seclusion until He had to come for fellowship or any pressing business as in **CHAPTER 11** still of the book of **GENESIS**.

GENESIS 11:1-9 KJV

And the whole earth was of one language, and of one speech. And it came to pass, as they journeyed from the east, that they found a plain in the land of Shinar; and they dwelt there. And they said one to another, Go to, let us make brick, and burn them throughly. And they had brick for stone, and slime had they for morter. And they said, Go to, let us build us a city and a tower, whose top may reach unto heaven; and let us make us a name, lest we be scattered abroad upon the face of the whole earth. And the LORD came down to see the city and the tower, which the children of men builded. And the LORD said, Behold, the people is one, and they have all one language; and this they begin to do: and now nothing will be restrained from them, which they have imagined to do. Go to, let us go down, and there confound their language, that they may not understand one another's speech. So the LORD scattered them abroad from thence upon the face of all the earth: and they left off to build the city. Therefore is the name of it called Babel; because the LORD did there confound the language of all the earth: and from thence did the LORD scatter them abroad upon the face of all the earth.

The account of the Tower of Babel does not teach us God separated us by languages just so that we may be dispersed. But also that He had to come down to see the tower. Meaning He was warned that in His absentia, the children of men are building a tower to reach heaven. So He had to come down to see it. So that He may adjudicate regarding the matter, meaning there were messengers relating the story to Him for Him to come down.

This account as a number of others that we shall use to relate, does not mean God is not all seeing. It means He created a veil between Him and the world, so that He may not see, by creating a seclusion that could contain His realm in to the Holy of Holies. He had no need to be contained in a tabernacle setting in heaven, but He did it so that He may be separated from the trial and redemption period of man. So that man may not sin in His presence.

Yet another sobering account that happened without God knowing on earth is the bedazzling of Sodom and Gomorrah, God had to go there to see if indeed, the sin of the inhabitants of this cities were indeed as wicked as He was told. Meaning He did not yet know, until that moment He had to come and see.

GENESIS 18:17-21 KJV

And the LORD said, Shall I hide from Abraham that thing which I do; Seeing that Abraham shall surely become a great and mighty nation, and all the nations of the earth shall be blessed in him? For I know him, that he will command his children and his household after him, and they shall keep the way of the LORD, to do justice and judgment; that the LORD may bring upon Abraham that which he hath spoken of him. And the LORD said, Because the cry of Sodom and Gomorrah is great, and because their sin is very grievous; I will go down now, and see whether they have done altogether according to the cry of it, which is come unto me; and if not, I will know.

The Lord, not the angels with Him says, "I will go and see if it is done altogether according to the cry..." meaning as the Lord stood in the presence of Abraham, He being the Lord did not know of the affairs of Sodom and Gomorrah. He yet had to see to attest to the aggravation of their sins.

Meaning the Lord was still in the business of separating Self, as they kept the memorial on earth.

Taking His sabbatical meant the Lord God by choice allowed man autonomy of the earthly realm. One other account is the account of satan in the book of Job. The Lord shows that He had not been aware of the matters of satan. Though the devil had been loitering the earth. Meaning the Lord was still in the seclusion to keep the Sabbath, so that man's mistakes may not happen in His presence before there is a Way or Order of redemption.

JOB 1:6-7 KJV

Now there was a day when the sons of God came to present themselves before the LORD, and Satan came also among them. And the LORD said unto Satan, Whence comest thou? Then Satan answered the LORD, and said, From going to and fro in the earth, and from walking up and down in it.

The above account shows that there was an elaborate system and a day when the sons of God; being the created angels had to bring report of the affairs of the world before God. Here the devil got the opportune moment where God stepped out of the Holiest to take report of His sons, of their wellbeing and the welfare of their service here on earth. The most important thing to consider is this meeting does not take place in heaven, considering the devil says in earth; meaning they are within the realm of the earth or he would have pointed earth as a distant place. So when he says in earth it gives the emphasis that the meeting is within the earth's realm.

This kind of report system is the mystery by which the devil found His way in to God's presence after he was cast out of heaven. Even though he has no place in heaven, in the earthly realm though judged, he is not yet subjected to his judgment, and by the **Principle of Approach** he can come before God though he has no portion in His glory.

When the tabernacle or tent of meeting was set here on earth, one thing the Lord did that one would say further mystified the Sabbath. For He would not appear to man, lest man would permanently be in His death. God made a shadow of the mercy seat, where without being seen, He could talk to the mediator of the Old Covenant being Moses the Judge.

EXODUS 25:22 KJV

And there I will meet with thee, and I will commune with thee from above the mercy seat, from between the two cherubims which are upon the ark of the testimony, of all things which I will give thee in commandment unto the children of Israel.

The mercy seat had to be in the replica of the Holy of Holies as is in heaven. And had to be upon the ark and in the midst of the cherubim, so that Moses may hear and not see God. Because God was in separation and should not be seen by man with the Adamic or sin nature as Moses, lest he saw Him and died.

EXODUS 33:20 KJV

And he said, Thou canst not see my face: for there shall no man see me, and live.

So the Sabbath is summed up as that time God took to separate Himself from man, so that He may not see man in his sin nature and death be man's permanent portion. One should know the emphasis is not on physical but spiritual death, just as in Eden. Until God had worked and finished a way of redemption. Then the redeemed man could boldly enter in to God's presence as the one who have defeated sin. And that is the complete reasoning behind the beginning and conclusion of Sabbath.

HEBREWS 10:19 KJV

Having therefore, brethren, boldness to enter into the holiest by the blood of Jesus,

NB: *The key reason being, if man had sinned in the presence of God, or the man with*

Adamic nature (as Moses) had appeared before God; because **God inhabits eternity***; man's sin would have been eternal making his fall permanent. That is to say the down fall of satan and all those who were under him was they sinned in the presence of God, so by principle their damnation is permanent. That is why they will never partake of a resurrection nor ever be mentioned anywhere in the things or plans of God. So God was saving us from this kind of doom by separating Himself and leaving us a day of memorial.*

ISAIAH 14:20-21 KJV

Thou shalt not be joined with them in burial, because thou hast destroyed thy land, and slain thy people: the seed of evildoers shall never be renowned. Prepare slaughter for his children for the iniquity of their fathers; that they do not rise, nor possess the land, nor fill the face of the world with cities.

The conclusion of the Sabbath

Mostly when we talk about the Sabbath, people automatically think the Old Testament (the Ten Commandments) and the word conclusion to them usually means destroyed, but it is no so. The Sabbath served its purpose and the Old Covenant served its purpose, both to a certain degree to keep us until a certain season or Order.

GALATIANS 4:1 KJV

Now I say, That the heir, as long as he is a child, differeth nothing from a servant, though he be lord of all; But is under tutors and governors until the time appointed of the father. Even so we, when we were children, were in bondage under the elements of the world: But when the fulness of the time was come, God sent forth his Son, made of a woman, made under the law, To redeem them that were under the law, that we might receive the adoption of sons.

According to the word of God, those who lived by the Law will be judged by the Law. That is why you will find the Ark of the Covenant in heaven even as we speak. Those who lived by that Law need it for their Abrahamic imputation of righteousness and to be judged according to the way they kept it.

REVELATION 11:19 KJV

And the temple of God was opened in heaven, and there was seen in his temple the ark of his testament: and there were lightnings, and voices, and thunderings, and an earthquake, and great hail.

REVELATION 5:1 KJV

And I saw in the right hand of him that sat on the throne a book written within and on the backside, sealed with seven seals.

So we do not just see the Covenant Box in the actual tabernacle of testimony in heaven, we even get to see the book that is written the words of both covenants that were given to man. God is seated next to the Covenant Box. So those who served under each Order will be judged by the statutes and judgments of that Order they served under, and that is why Christ did not come to destroy the Law but to fulfill what is written of Him in it.

HEBREWS 9:16-17 KJV

For where a testament is, there must also of necessity be the death of the testator. For a testament is of force after men are dead: otherwise it is of no strength at all while the testator liveth.

In a simpler interpretation of the above statement, one would understand that the same word Testament, is the very same word Will. In simple terms you cannot act on anyone's will until they are dead. For until they are dead they need their estate and goods to make a living.

 In continuation, God did not just reward His only begotten son, but caused Him in the total man to take the seat that its desire caused the devil to fall. In the glorified incarnate Christ Jesus, man is seated in the highest place of honor as our Lord seats as both the total man and the total God upon the throne of the Father. So Apostle Paul confesses.

EPHESIANS 2:6 KJV

And hath raised us up together, and made us sit together in heavenly places in Christ Jesus:

In essence, from the point He presented His blood and sat beside the Father, He awaited us to enter in to His rest, not as the original that separated God from us, but the new that separates us from the world in to His presence. So when we are done with the errands and Great Commission in this world, we go and get in to His rest.

When we talk about the conclusion of the Sabbath, we begin to hear a new term in the New Testament that resonates from the old;

rest. David so much mentions entering in to the rest of God as a prophetic word. When all were looking for a way to get out of the Sabbath, He prophesied of something beyond the Stone Covenant and the Melchisedec Order, he talks of eternal rest in the tabernacle of testimony. But yet He talks of those who failed to enter this eternal rest of God because of unbelief.

PSALMS 95:10-11 KJV

Forty years long was I grieved with this generation, and said, It is a people that do err in their heart, and they have not known my ways: Unto whom I sware in my wrath that they should not enter into my rest.

JOHN 5:17-18 KJV

But Jesus answered them, My Father worketh hitherto, and I work. Therefore the Jews sought the more to kill him, because he not only had broken the sabbath, but said also that God was his Father, making himself equal with God.

In God standing with Christ in His ministry, He just knew He had to show the world what the manifest sons should be like, the Father was already in the business of restoring man, by being with Him in all His works. For all the works and the teachings He had to teach were from the Father, not written ordinances of works of the Law. The Father was already engaged in the restoration of man through His only begotten. And the son also was already calling His brothers in to His rest.

MATTHEW 11:28-29 KJV

Come unto me, all ye that labour and are heavy laden, and I will give you rest. Take my yoke upon you, and learn of me; for I am meek and lowly in heart: and ye shall find rest unto your souls.

JOHN 5:19 KJV

Then answered Jesus and said unto them, Verily, verily, I say unto you, The Son can do nothing of himself, but what he seeth the Father do: for what things soever he doeth, these also doeth the Son likewise.

The engagement of God in the business of the earth is back on through the son, but those who observe the day of separation as a commemoration they are still holding on. Essentially because they kept it as a Law from Moses not by God's revelation.

This teaches us why we have to be so respectful and reverence God as our Father. For until Christ began His ministry, from the first day that He finished His work on earth, He had to be in self isolation so that we may not sin in His presence. As a Father would do for His children, even when we had lost our sonship.

PSALMS 103:13 KJV

Like as a father pitieth his children, so the LORD pitieth them that fear him.

He secluded His omnipresence and His omnipotence in to captivity until man was in a position where he could be restored if he falls. He that had been sitting in separation or seclusion through the ages since **GENESIS**

2:3, begins to prepare and do things that the son does. For He had sent the son to do His works in those three and half years of His incarnate ministry, it engages the Father for the son to do anything. The less careful in the spirit do not see the Father much here, but for the man Jesus Christ to do anything, He had to be enabled by the Father through His Spirit.

So those who kept the Sabbath as tradition asked Him and yet they failed to comprehend. That the works that He did were not His but from the one who sent Him, here it simply means even before His death and resurrection the Father was already back in the affairs of this world. That is why when Philip asks to see the Father Jesus Christ tells Him, when you have seen me you have seen the Father, for it is the Father that is behind all the words and the works that I do.

JOHN 14:9-11 KJV

Jesus saith unto him, Have I been so long

time with you, and yet hast thou not known me, Philip? he that hath seen me hath seen the Father; and how sayest thou then, Shew us the Father? Believest thou not that I am in the Father, and the Father in me? the words that I speak unto you I speak not of myself: but the Father that dwelleth in me, he doeth the works. Believe me that I am in the Father, and the Father in me: or else believe me for the very works' sake.

By the time He presents His blood, the manifest work of seclusion was under foot. Man was already walking on redemption but the whole righteousness had to be fulfilled. What He had been doing through messengers like Moses and other prophets of the Old, He was ready to send the Holy Spirit to dwell in all His children. So that the Spirit may be their Help and edification that is God now joined back to man (out of Self separation) and it announces the end of the earthly and heavenly Sabbath.

JOHN 16:13-15 KJV

Howbeit when he, the Spirit of truth, is come, he will guide you into all truth: for he shall not speak of himself; but whatsoever he shall hear, that shall he speak: and he will shew you things to come. He shall glorify me: for he shall receive of mine, and shall shew it unto you. All things that the Father hath are mine: therefore said I, that he shall take of mine, and shall shew it unto you.

MARK 16:17-18 KJV

And these signs shall follow them that believe; In my name shall they cast out devils; they shall speak with new tongues; They shall take up serpents; and if they drink any deadly thing, it shall not hurt them; they shall lay hands on the sick, and they shall recover.

Sincerely, the most profound thing is as God has come to earth to be with us in our earthly pilgrim so we too long to be with Him in His heavenly place of rest. We get anguished and desire so much to be in His eternal presence. The same tabernacle that separated Him from us is the same tabernacle we desire to be among us. For when it is among us we shall rest from all our sorrows, our sickness and hunger, that is the place of our eternal rest, that's the ultimate resting place.

REVELATION 21:3-7 KJV

And I heard a great voice out of heaven saying, Behold, the tabernacle of God is with men, and he will dwell with them, and they shall be his people, and God himself shall be with them, and be their God. And God shall wipe away all tears from their eyes; and there shall be no more death, neither sorrow, nor crying, neither shall there be any more pain: for the former things are passed away. And he that sat upon the throne said, Behold, I make all things new. And he said unto me, Write: for these words are true and faithful. And he said unto me, It is done. I am Alpha and Omega, the beginning and the end. I will give unto him that is athirst of the fountain of the water of life freely. He that overcometh shall inherit all things; and I will be his God, and he shall be my son.

Where no human being, but only the priest of God had been allowed before because of the Sabbath, we are now allowed and we have a way of redemption in case we sin. The Father having accomplished it through Christ. So now we go in to His room of separation (Sabbath) to rest as the Lord Jesus Christ promises us His rest as a sure future for our lives, that if we would hold to the profession of our faith we will also sit with Him upon His throne as after being able to conquer (to reap the veil of the Sabbath), His Father allowed Him to sit with Him upon His throne.

REVELATION 3:21 KJV

To him that overcometh will I grant to sit with me in my throne, even as I also overcame, and am set down with my Father in his throne.

What began as a place of solitude for God the Father in Sabbath, is now a place of increase in Jesus Christ and that is the conclusion of the Sabbath. So that we may enter His eternal rest.

SINNER'S PRAYER TO RECEIVE JESUS AS SAVIOR

If you are not saved please pray this prayer...

Dear Heavenly Father I come to You in The Name of Jesus Christ. Your Word says, "37 All that the Father giveth me shall come to me; and him that cometh to me I will in no wise cast out."

JOHN 6:37

So I know You will not cast me out, but You take me in and I thank You for that. You said in your Word, "13 For whosoever shall call upon the name of the Lord shall be saved."

ROMANS 10:13

You also said in Your Word, "9 That if thou shalt confess with thy mouth the Lord Jesus, and shalt believe in thine heart that God hath raised him from the dead, thou shalt be saved. 10 For with the heart man believeth unto righteousness; and with the mouth confession is made unto salvation."

ROMANS 10:9-10

I believe in my heart Jesus Christ is the son of God. I believe that He was raised from the dead for my justification

And I am saved, thank You Lord!

OTHER BOOKS BY THE SAME AUTHOR:

TRANSLATIONS TO OTHER LANGUAGES:

Baptismo to Kolobetso – **Setswana**